Decodable Takehome Books

Level B Set 2

A Division of The McGraw-Hill Companies

Columbus, Ohio

SRA/McGraw-Hill

A Division of The **McGraw·Hill** *Companies*

Printed in the United States of America.

Send all inquiries to:
SRA/McGraw-Hill
4400 Easton Commons
Columbus, OH 43219

ISBN 0-02-683933-4

17 18 19 20 QPD 10 09

Contents

About the Decodable Takehome Books

The *SRA Open Court Reading Decodable Books* allow your students to apply their knowledge of phonic elements to read simple, engaging texts. Each story supports instruction in a new phonic element and incorporates elements and words that have been learned earlier.

The students can fold and staple the pages of each *Decodable Takehome Book* to make books of their own to keep and read. We suggest that you keep extra sets of the stories in your classroom for the children to reread.

How to make a Decodable Takehome Book

1. Tear out the pages you need.

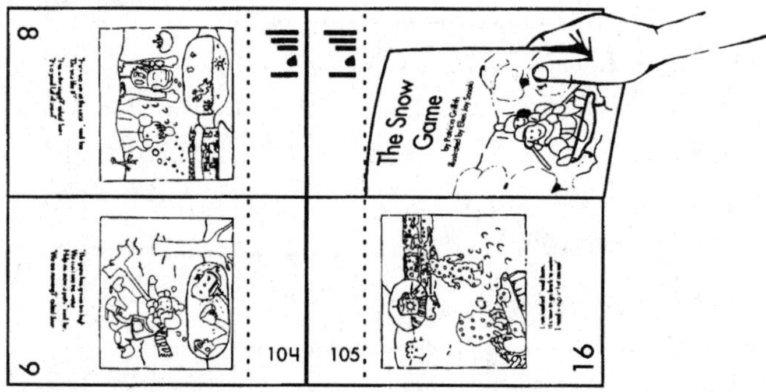

2. For 16-page stories, place pages 8 and 9, 6 and 11, 4 and 13, and 2 and 15 faceup.

3. Place the pages on top of each other in this order: pages 8 and 9, pages 6 and 11, pages 4 and 13, and pages 2 and 15.

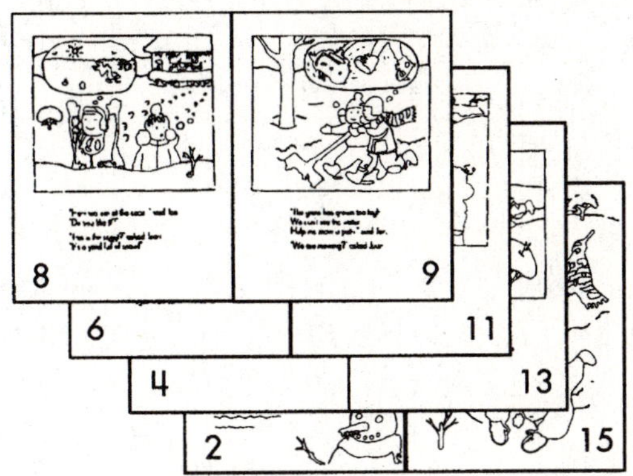

4. Fold along the center line.

5. Check to make sure the pages are in order.

6. Staple the pages along the fold.

Just to let you know...

A message from ____

Help your child discover the joy of independent reading with *SRA Open Court Reading.* From time to time your child will bring home his or her very own *Decodable Takehome Books* to share with you. With your help, these stories can give your child important reading practice and a joyful shared reading experience.

You may want to set aside a few minutes every evening to read these stories together. Here are some suggestions you may find helpful:

- Do not expect your child to read each story perfectly, but concentrate on sharing the book together.
- Participate by doing some of the reading.
- Talk about the stories as you read, give lots of encouragement, and watch as your child becomes more fluent throughout the year!

Learning to read takes lots of practice. Sharing these stories is one way that your child can gain that valuable practice. Encourage your child to keep the *Decodable Takehome Books* in a special place. This collection will make a library of books that your child can read and reread. Take the time to listen to your child read from his or her library. Just a few moments of shared reading each day can give your child the confidence needed to excel in reading.

Children who read every day come to think of reading as a pleasant, natural part of life. One way to inspire your child to read is to show that reading is an important part of your life by letting him or her see you reading books, magazines, newspapers, or any other materials. Another good way to show that you value reading is to share a *Decodable Takehome Book* with your child each day.

Successful reading experiences allow children to be proud of their new-found reading ability. Support your child with interest and enthusiasm about reading. You won't regret it!

Pam sits with Sam.
Everyone loves Sam and Pam.

Open Court Reading

Everyone Loves Pam and Sam

by Aleta Naylor
illustrated by Kersti Frigell

A Division of The McGraw-Hill Companies
Columbus, Ohio

SRA/McGraw-Hill

A Division of The ***McGraw·Hill*** *Companies*

Printed in the United States of America.

Send all inquiries to:
SRA/McGraw-Hill
8787 Orion Place
Columbus, OH 43240-4027

Sam is not sad and mad.
Pam is not sad and mad.
Sam nods and Mom pats him.
Mom and Dad pat Pam.

Grandma Dot tells Pam that Sam is not sad and mad. All babies cry. It is not bad.

Baby Sam

Sam is Pam's baby brother.

20

Sam nods and naps.
Pam nods and naps.

Can you help Sam?

Pam spots Grandma Dot
and Grandpa Stan.

Sam holds Mom's hand.
Pam holds Dad's hand.

22

Mom pats and taps Sam.
Pam pats and taps Mom.

Pam stands and calls for Dad.
Dad can not help.

Pam stops and taps Mom.
Mom can not help.

Sam sits with Dad and sips.
Pam sits and sips.

Pam sits and is sad.

24

Pam and Sam

Sam is sad and sobs.
Can someone help?

Rick: Pam, we are stuck in mud. Stop and help us. Grab rugs, mats, or socks. But do not pick up rocks or sticks!

SRA

Open Court Reading

Stuck!

by Lisa Trumbauer
illustrated by Len Epstein

SRA

A Division of The McGraw-Hill Companies

Columbus, Ohio

26

SRA/McGraw-Hill

A Division of The McGraw-Hill Companies

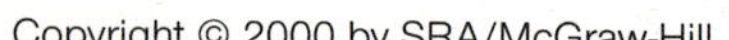

Printed in the United States of America.

Send all inquiries to:
SRA/McGraw-Hill
8787 Orion Place
Columbus, OH 43240-4027

Rob Rabbit trips! Bob Bug, Don Duck, Rob Rabbit, and Rick are all stuck back in mud.

Rick: Rob Rabbit, tug Don Duck.
Don Duck, tug Bob Bug.
Bob Bug, tug on my hand.

Stuck in Mud

Bob Bug is stuck.
Bob Bug is stuck in mud.

Don Duck is stuck.
Don Duck is stuck in mud.
Don Duck and Bob Bug are stuck in mud.

Rob Rabbit: Don Duck, grab Bob Bug.
Bob Bug, grab Rick's hand.

Rob Rabbit: His stick is stuck in mud!
Don Duck: Bob Bug, tug on
Rick's hand.

Rob Rabbit is stuck in mud.
Rob Rabbit is stuck with Don Duck and
Bob Bug.

Rick sees Bob Bug, Don Duck, and Rob Rabbit stuck in mud.

Rick

Bob Bug, Don Duck, and Rob Rabbit: Rick is stuck in mud! Let's get his big stick.

Bob Bug pops up. Don Duck runs up.
Rob Rabbit hops up.
Rick dips back in the mud.

Rick: Bob Bug, hop up on a rock!
Rob Rabbit, run and grab a rock!
Bob Bug: Don Duck is still stuck in mud.

Rob Rabbit: Let's get Don Duck.
Rick: Bob Bug, Don Duck, and Rob Rabbit are stuck back in mud.

Bob Bug: Rick, pick up a big stick.
Rick: Grab on the stick.
Don Duck: Rick, tug the stick!

33

Big Bill and Little Bill sit on a mat.
Big Bill is not too big, and Little Bill is not too little.
Big Bill and Little Bill are still best friends.

SRA
Open Court Reading

Big Bill and Little Bill

by Aleta Naylor
illustrated by Len Epstein

A Division of The McGraw-Hill Companies
Columbus, Ohio

SRA/McGraw-Hill

A Division of The McGraw·Hill Companies

Printed in the United States of America.

Send all inquiries to:
SRA/McGraw-Hill
8787 Orion Place
Columbus, OH 43240-4027

34

What can Big Bill and Little Bill do? Where can they sit and snack, nap, and jump?

Big Bill and Little Bill jump.
But Big Bill is too big.
Big Bill bumps his head.

Little Bill in a Big House

Big Bill and Little Bill are best friends.
Big Bill asks if Little Bill can come over.

Big Bill and Little Bill sit.
But Little Bill is too little.
Little Bill slips off.

Big Bill and Little Bill nap.
But Big Bill is too big.
Big Bill falls off the edge.

Big Bill and Little Bill snack.
But Big Bill is too big.
Big Bill flips his fudge.

Big Bill and Little Bill snack.
But Little Bill is too little.
Little Bill can't jump up.

Big Bill and Little Bill nap.
But Little Bill is too little.
Little Bill flips over the edge.

Big Bill and Little Bill sit.
But Big Bill is too big.
Big Bill cracks the back.

39

Big Bill in a Little House

Little Bill and Big Bill are best friends.
Little Bill asks if Big Bill can come over.

Big Bill and Little Bill like fast spins.
But Little Bill is too little.
Little Bill spins off into the hedge.

What can Little Bill and Big Bill do?
Where can they sit and snack,
nap, and spin?

"Zack, you napped all night!"

SRA

Open Court Reading

Zack's Nap

by Kristen Salvatore
illustrated by Gary Undercuffler

A Division of The McGraw-Hill Companies

Columbus, Ohio

SRA/McGraw-Hill

A Division of The **McGraw·Hill** *Companies*

Printed in the United States of America.

Send all inquiries to:
SRA/McGraw-Hill
8787 Orion Place
Columbus, OH 43240-4027

At last Zack jumps off his bed.
"Mom, didn't I just nap a bit?"

43

Zack did not budge from his bed's edge.

Time for Bed

Zack's mom says, "It's past time for bed. Let's turn off TV."
Zack did not budge.

"But, Mom," grumbles Zack,
"this act has not ended."

"Mom, can I rest a bit more?
Didn't I just hop in bed?"

“It’s time to get up, Zack.
Get scrubbed and dressed!”

Zack stands up, and his mom
sends him on his way.

Zack stands at his sink. "Mom, I'm not sleepy. Can I stay up for just six more minutes?"

Time to Wake Up

"Zack, it is half past six. The sun is up."

“Mom, don’t click off the lamp.
Let me read more on foxes.”

Zack’s mom hands him a soap bar.
“It fizzes and forms suds as you scrub.
It is fun.”

Zack stops as he passes the TV.
"There is a big net if she slips."

Zack sits up in his bed. His mom
puts an extra blanket on Zack's bed.

Then her mom rushes in
and grins a big grin.
"That was an extra long bath!
You are a big girl, Beth!"

SRA

Open Court Reading

A Bath for Beth

by Dina McClellean
illustrated by Jan Pyk

A Division of The McGraw-Hill Companies

Columbus, Ohio

SRA/McGraw-Hill

A Division of The **McGraw-Hill** *Companies*

Printed in the United States of America.

Send all inquiries to:
SRA/McGraw-Hill
8787 Orion Place
Columbus, OH 43240-4027

Beth hops in her tub.
Beth scrubs and scrubs.
Then she steps out.
"BETH!" her mom calls.
"I'm finished," Beth says.

Beth puts dishes, cups, wax lips, the sax, and fish on her mat. Beth gets them all picked out as fast as she can!

Beth Has Fun

"Beth, Beth! Get in that bath!"

"Yes, Mom!" Beth says,
"after I put all these up.
Then I'll hop in this tub
and scrub and scrub!"

Beth picks the box,
the fox, pigs, and an ox!

53

Beth Has Her Bath

"BETH, BETH, DID YOU FINISH THAT BATH?"

Water rushes and gushes
from Beth's bath tap.
Bubbles hiss and sizzle and plop.
They fizzle until they pop.

"Beth, Beth! GET IN THAT BATH!"
On the bath mat is a zigzag path.
Beth sits on that mat and has fun.

Dishes, cups, and fish—
Beth mixes them all up.

Beth drops fish with fins in next.

"Beth, Beth! DID YOU GET IN THAT BATH?" Beth picks up the box and the little red fox. The box and fox make big splashes as Beth drops them in her bath. Next Beth drops in pigs and an ox.

Beth adds dishes and
cups, for six,

red wax lips, and a sax
to her mix in her bath.

"No, we still make fudge by hand. It is not fast, but it is fun!"

SRA

Open Court Reading

Midge at the Farm

by Yve Knick
illustrated by Meryl Henderson

A Division of The McGraw-Hill Companies

Columbus, Ohio

SRA/McGraw-Hill

A Division of The **McGraw·Hill** *Companies*

Printed in the United States of America.

Send all inquiries to:
SRA/McGraw-Hill
8787 Orion Place
Columbus, OH 43240-4027

"Can you help us with this fudge, Midge?" ask Gran and Gramps.

"Aren't there machines for that?" mumbles Midge.

"I can't help Gran and Gramps.
This is not fun."

Farm Fun

"It is fun at Gran and Gramp's farm, Midge. When I was little, I helped them. Farm jobs are fun."

"I helped Gramps plant his garden, Midge. We chopped and tilled big patches of land. Then Gramps and I dropped in seeds."

"Gramps, can I help pick vegetables?"

"Vegetables are not picked by hand, Midge. This garden is just too big. Machines help pick vegetables. It is fast."

"Gran, can I help milk cows?"

"Cows are not milked by hand, Midge. Machines pump fresh milk into big tubs. Then it gets pumped into jugs. It is fast."

"I helped Gran collect eggs, Midge. As hens scratched in pens, we picked eggs from hens' nests."

"I helped Gran milk her cows, Midge. Then at lunch, Gran, Gramps, and I sipped chilled milk in big, tall glasses. It was fun!"

"Gran, can I help collect eggs?"

"The eggs are not collected by hand, Midge. There are just too many hens. Machines collect the eggs. It is fast."

Fast Farm

"Gramps, can I help plant this garden?"

"The garden is not planted by hand, Midge. This garden is just too big. Machines chop and till and plant seeds. It is fast."

"I helped Gramps pick vegetables, Midge. We'd rinse them off and then munch and crunch them for snacks."

"I helped Gran and Gramps make fudge with fresh eggs and milk that we collected. Mmmmm! It was such rich fudge!"

"Just past that bridge is the farm! There are Gran and Gramps on the porch. They are glad to see us."

Chirp missed that impish, speckled cat. Now Chirp spends time with his best pal, Scat.

SRA Open Court Reading

Chirp and Scat

by Toby Gates
illustrated by Len Epstein

A Division of The McGraw-Hill Companies
Columbus, Ohio

SRA/McGraw-Hill

A Division of The ***McGraw-Hill*** *Companies*

Printed in the United States of America.

Send all inquiries to:
SRA/McGraw-Hill
8787 Orion Place
Columbus, OH 43240-4027

Chirp admitted that he'd not been fair, and Chirp felt bad that Scat was put out there.

"Scat, that's it. Get out!" Robert said.
Then Chirp felt bad.
In fact Chirp felt sad.
Scat whimpered and got up from his soft bed.

Scat Moves In

Chirp is a bird.
Scat is a cat.
Chirp and Scat live with Robert and Bertha Platt.

Wind was hitting fast and hard
when Scat turned up in Platt's backyard.

Next Chirp tugged and scratched at Platt's rug.
The Platts stepped in and spotted Scat, all snug.

Chirp was glad his plan had worked.
Chirp jumped, fluttered, and chirped.

Scat was such an impish little cat.
Robert and Bertha called him Scat.

Scat turned fast for such an impish cat.
Robert and Bertha loved Scat's purr
when they sat.

Robert hollered at Scat for scratching
Bertha's chair.
Scat sat puzzled and felt this was not fair.

Chirp flipped his latch back and sat on his perch.
Chirp laughed at Scat left there in a lurch.

Robert and Bertha could not tell that Chirp did not like Scat very well.

Did Bertha and Robert forget Chirp at last?
Chirp felt that Scat must exit rather fast!

Chirp's Plan

Chirp started his plan and lifted his latch. Chirp went to Bertha's chair and scratched at the patch.

I left the big tent with my pal Kate. That circus was grand and all acts were first rate.

SRA
Open Court Reading

Circus

by Tamera Bryant
illustrated by Olivia Cole

A Division of The McGraw-Hill Companies

Columbus, Ohio

SRA/McGraw-Hill

A Division of The McGraw-Hill Companies

Printed in the United States of America.

Send all inquiries to:
SRA/McGraw-Hill
8787 Orion Place
Columbus, OH 43240-4027

Chimps came in next for quick skate races.
They raced in circles and quickly changed places.
The chimps made us giggle and made such a sight.
Then the ringmaster stepped in to tell us good night.

Then came a cannon with a man getting in. As he slid further in we saw cannon man's grin.

It flared and flamed. It blared and it blazed. When cannon man blasted off, we all felt dazed.

Getting In

I went to a circus with a pal named Kate. We ran up a path to a big circus gate.

Kate and I jumped to glance over a fence. Then we dug in big pockets for our last ten cents.

Then jugglers with big plates entered the tent. They tossed plates up fast, and then off they went.

Back and forth they passed and met.
I relaxed when they landed safe in a net.

With big bags of snacks and
glad faces, we ran into a tent
and got our places.

As we were sitting, we started wiggling.
It's hard sitting still when we start giggling.

We did not squirm or flinch.
They swung and grabbed thin bars.
We did not shift an inch, as we gazed
at these circus stars.

Acrobats swung up with such reckless daring.
Kate and I sat in our places just staring.

A band with drums started playing songs.
We sat still and hushed as others sang along.

Center Ring

The ringmaster came in with a long,
black cape.
It had big red spots in different shapes.
Taking her place in the center ring,
she tells us things the circus will bring:
acrobats, big cats, cannons that blast,
clowns, jugglers, and chimps that are fast.

The first act came on—two big lions so tame.
They ran in a circle and jumped across
a flame.

Clowns ran in with big rubber snakes
and tossed buckets filled with paper flakes.

Now Cat can do things in his hat.
Cat walks off and waves his thanks to Bat.

SRA
Open Court Reading

Cat and His Hat

by Dennis Andersen
illustrated by Pat Lucas-Morris

A Division of The McGraw-Hill Companies
Columbus, Ohio

SRA/McGraw-Hill

A Division of The **McGraw-Hill** *Companies*

Printed in the United States of America.

Send all inquiries to:
SRA/McGraw-Hill
8787 Orion Place
Columbus, OH 43240-4027

Bat adds a wide red sash.
This will help keep Cat's hat in place.

"Yes! Yes! I like this hat," yells Cat.
Bat has fixed Cat's problem hat!

Cat's Problem Hat

This is Cat.
Cat does not like his hat.
Cat has a problem with his hat.
Can anyone help?

Cat can't see and steps in a mud hole.
Cat has a problem with his hat.
Can anyone help?

Bat puts more feathers in a
circle on Cat's hat.
Will this fix Cat's problem hat?

93

Bat puts a bigger feather in the center.
Will this fix Cat's problem hat?

Cat can't sip a drink when his hat is on his head.
Cat has a problem with his hat.
Can anyone help?

Cat can't take hikes in his hat.
Cat has a problem with his hat.
Can anyone help?

Bat puts a little feather on Cat's hat.
Will this fix Cat's problem hat?

Bat Helps Cat

Cat tells Bat he has a problem hat.
Bat tells Cat he can help fix that.

SRA
Open Court
Reading

Cat can't ride a bike in his hat.
Cat has a problem with his hat.
Can anyone help?

Cat stops and thinks. Can his problem with his hat be fixed?

Perhaps Bat can fix his problem hat.

This big city is not the same as home,
but I still like it.
A big city is full of nice surprises.

SRA Open Court Reading

A Trip to the City

by Aleta Naylor
illustrated by Len Epstein

A Division of The McGraw-Hill Companies
Columbus, Ohio

SRA/McGraw-Hill

A Division of The **McGraw·Hill** *Companies*

Printed in the United States of America.

Send all inquiries to:
SRA/McGraw-Hill
8787 Orion Place
Columbus, OH 43240-4027

This is a nice surprise! No one is scared.
Everyone shares to help make things better.

Oh, no! The subway has stopped.
Is it time to get off?
I'm a bit scared.

A Letter

Please come and see us. Our home is in a big city. We can explore exciting places and do fun things. Hope you will say yes.

I am a little scared, but I think it will be fun.
Mom tells me a city is full of nice things.

This is a subway.
It is so fast and quick.
I am surprised that I am not scared.
I think this will be fun!

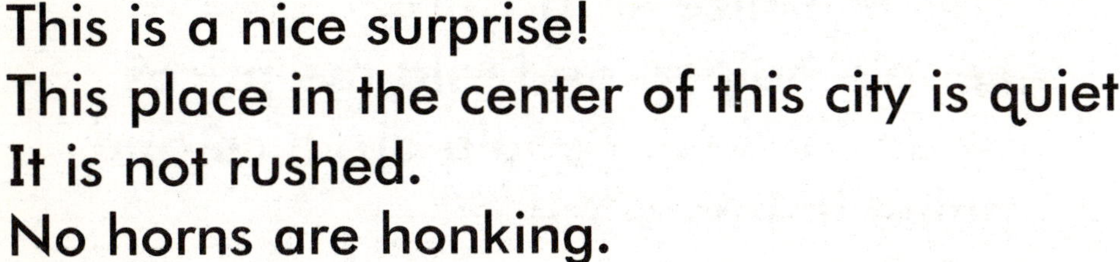

This is a nice surprise!
This place in the center of this city is quiet.
It is not rushed.
No horns are honking.

I hope I will not get bumped and cramped.
At home there is a lot more space.
But Mom tells me a city has nice things.

I hope someone will tell me prices when I ask.
At home everyone is nice and polite.
But Mom tells me a city is full of nice things.

This is a nice surprise!
People helped and told me prices when I asked. People are nice and polite in this place.

A Big City

This is a nice surprise!
I am not bumped and cramped.
That man can even ride his bike.

I hope car horns do not blare and honk so much there. At home horns do not honk at all.
But Mom tells me a city has nice things.

I hope I will not get scared riding on a subway.
At home there is no subway.
But Mom tells me a city has nice things.

I see so much cement and so many faces.
Everything rushes at such quick paces.

Pete was at the vet with Dad.
Steve has found his pal Pete!

SRA Open Court Reading

Where Is Pete?

by Kristen Salvatore
illustrated by Gary Undercuffler

SRA

A Division of The McGraw-Hill Companies

Columbus, Ohio

SRA/McGraw-Hill

A Division of The ***McGraw-Hill*** *Companies*

Printed in the United States of America.

Send all inquiries to:
SRA/McGraw-Hill
8787 Orion Place
Columbus, OH 43240-4027

The clock strikes five, and here is Dad. Pete is with Dad!

The clue on Dad's note says,
"*We* went to the vet."
Someone went with Dad.
Did Pete go with Dad?

Where Is Pete?

Steve likes to play with his pal, Pete.
Steve decides to find Pete.
But Steve cannot find Pete.
Where is Pete?

Is Pete in Mom's large van?

It is a clue!
Dad's note is a clue.

No, he is not in Mom's van.

Is Pete under blue and white covers?

What is on this desk?
It's a note.
It's a note that Dad wrote.

A Clue

Steve looked in Mom's van and under blue and white covers. He looked in the kitchen. Where is Pete?

No, he is not under blue and white covers.

Is Pete fixing tuna and gingersnaps, the snacks he likes best?

No, he is not fixing tuna and gingersnaps.

Now the peanut butter's famous.
This peanut butter saved us.
Peanut butter is the best!

SRA

Open Court Reading

Peanut Butter Is the Best!

by Lisa Trumbauer
illustrated by Jan Pyk

A Division of The McGraw-Hill Companies

Columbus, Ohio

SRA/McGraw-Hill

A Division of The **McGraw-Hill** *Companies*

Printed in the United States of America.

Send all inquiries to:
SRA/McGraw-Hill
8787 Orion Place
Columbus, OH 43240-4027

At last my family can see.
At last they finally agree.
Peanut butter is the best!

Peanut butter is so dandy.
Peanut butter comes in handy.
Peanut butter is the best!

I Love Peanut Butter

Peanut butter—it is creamy.
Peanut butter—it is dreamy.
Peanut butter is the best!

It is better than canned ham.
It is better than sweet jam.
Peanut butter is the best!

Oh no! It's a skunk. Pee-ew!
She likes peanut butter, too.
Peanut butter is the best!

Here comes an insect, bird, and rabbit.
They like it, but they can't have it.
Peanut butter is the best!

It glides so easily on a slice.
That makes peanut butter nice.
Peanut butter is the best!

I will pack it in a sack.
I will pack it for a snack.
Peanut butter is the best!

Yes, he does. I believe it's true.
He likes peanut butter, too.
Peanut butter is the best!

See that squirrel sitting behind Mother?
I'll bet he's looking for peanut butter.
Peanut butter is the best!

You may pack it with the rest,
but peanut butter's still the best.
Peanut butter is the best!

Peanut butter beats your jelly.
Peanut butter sticks to your belly.
Peanut butter is the best!

They Love Peanut Butter

When it is spread on extra thick,
I even like it on a celery stick.
Peanut butter is the best!

As Kay steps out of the bank,
a large gust of wind rushes past her.
Her hat is lifted off her head.
This time Kay stands and waves good-bye!

SRA Open Court Reading

Pat the Cat and Kay's Hat

by Truman Vega
illustrated by Jan Pyk

A Division of The McGraw-Hill Companies
Columbus, Ohio

SRA/McGraw-Hill

A Division of The McGraw-Hill Companies

Printed in the United States of America.

Send all inquiries to:
SRA/McGraw-Hill
8787 Orion Place
Columbus, OH 43240-4027

"This cash is nice," states Kay, "but I will share. I will split this cash with Officer Bopp and Pat. We are glad we could help catch that rat."

The bank president thanks Kay and gives her cash.
"Your smart hat put an end to that thief.
That rat robbed so many banks."

Wind Catches Hat

Pat the Cat stops his cab so
he can sneak a nap.
He blocks the light
by pulling down his cap.
Then he closes his eyes tight.

Just then Kay steps out.
A large gust of wind rushes by her.
The wind lifts Kay's hat off her head.
Kay yells, "That wind has my hat!"

Officer Bopp is happy as he holds the rat in a cage. He tells Pat and Kay, "That hat trapped the rat that robbed a bank. That is a smart hat!"

"My hat is back! This is a lucky day," squeals Kay. "I'm pleased that chase has ended."
Kay places her hat back on her head.

Kay runs to Pat's parked cab
and quickly opens the back door.
She calls to Pat,
"Chase that hat! Make it fast!"

Pat starts his cab and chases Kay's hat.
Pat and Kay drive on main streets.
Kay's hat stays in the air.
Her hat just will not fall down.

Hat Catches Rat

But just as Kay had lost all hope, her hat drops down. It lands on a large rat with a mask. A rat is trapped under Kay's hat!

If hats talked, this hat would say,
"How dull is this life I've led!
You can't catch me!
I feel so free when I'm not on Kay's head."

Just then Officer Bopp rides up and orders Pat to stop his cab.
But Kay asks from the back,
"Oh, can you help us, Officer Bopp?"

Behind Kay's hat is Pat's cab and Officer Bopp on his horse. Next come a van, a cart, and a bus.
Kay's hat has a head start and takes a quick turn.
Kay believes her hat is lost.

I fly right home, and I land in my bed,
with memories of flying still in my head.

SRA Open Court Reading

Dream Night

by Lisa Trumbauer
illustrated by Mark Corcoran

A Division of The McGraw·Hill Companies

Columbus, Ohio

Open Court Reading

SRA/McGraw-Hill

A Division of The ***McGraw-Hill*** *Companies*

Printed in the United States of America.

Send all inquiries to:
SRA/McGraw-Hill
8787 Orion Place
Columbus, OH 43240-4027

A new day is coming, I'd better hurry. If I'm not home by sunrise, my mom will be worried.

"I win!" yells Queen Sky, and we give a big cheer.
Then I say so long. The sun's nearly here.

Dream Flight

I close my eyes. I shut them tight.
I hold them closed with all my might.

I wish I may, I wish I might
dream a dream this same night.

I try to dream. As I'm trying,
suddenly, I feel I'm flying.

We tiptoe over daisies, run up steep stairs,
slide down a long tube, then sit on chairs.

We row little boats around stars in the sky.
Then we each chew a piece of a blueberry pie.

I'm flying high. I'm out my window.
I see bright stars and feel winds blow.

I am dreaming. I can fly over trees and in blue sky.

Then Sue, Blue, and I run a race with Queen Sky, a race unlike any that I've ever seen.

"Happy Tuesday! My name is Sue.
This is my mom and our puppy named Blue."

Sue's mom is a queen on a queenly throne.
She asks if I'd like an ice-cream cone.

I soar up high, then glide back down.
I fly up again and far from town.

Dream Place

I see a place, all bright and shiny.
Then a girl flies right by me!

This girl flies and flies with flair.
She can do handstands in midair!

She flies like a butterfly, fancy and free,
dipping and floating and smiling at me.

Everyone claps for our play.
We did just fine.
This is our big night!

SRA Open Court Reading

School Play

by Lisa Trumbauer
illustrated by Meryl Henderson

A Division of The McGraw-Hill Companies
Columbus, Ohio

SRA/McGraw-Hill

A Division of The **McGraw·Hill** *Companies*

Printed in the United States of America.

Send all inquiries to:
SRA/McGraw-Hill
8787 Orion Place
Columbus, OH 43240-4027

We say the lines on cue!
We say them right!

We sing a few songs!
We ring many bells!

Getting Set

We have a lot to do for a school play.
There are many things to get ready.

We paint sets for scenes.
We make props.

Okay! It is time!
It is time for the play!

Will I remember my lines?
Will I say them on cue?

We shine all of the spotlights.
The stage must be swept.

Parts are practiced.
Lines need memorized.

We tied things on tight.
We have roles to play.

We swept the stage.
We set the stage.

We practice singing a few songs.
We practice ringing tunes with bells.

We have a stage to set and things to tie on tight.

The Big Night

My school is performing a play! Tonight is the night!

145

Stu was not outside.
He was not at the lake.
Stu was in my house
eating birthday cake!"

SRA
Open Court Reading

Loose Goose

by Marilee Robin Burton
illustrated by Deborah Colvin Borgo

A Division of The McGraw-Hill Companies
Columbus, Ohio

SRA Open Court Reading

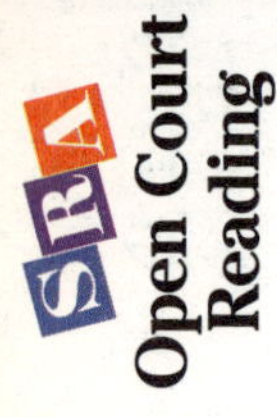

SRA/McGraw-Hill
A Division of The McGraw-Hill Companies

Printed in the United States of America.

Send all inquiries to:
SRA/McGraw-Hill
8787 Orion Place
Columbus, OH 43240-4027

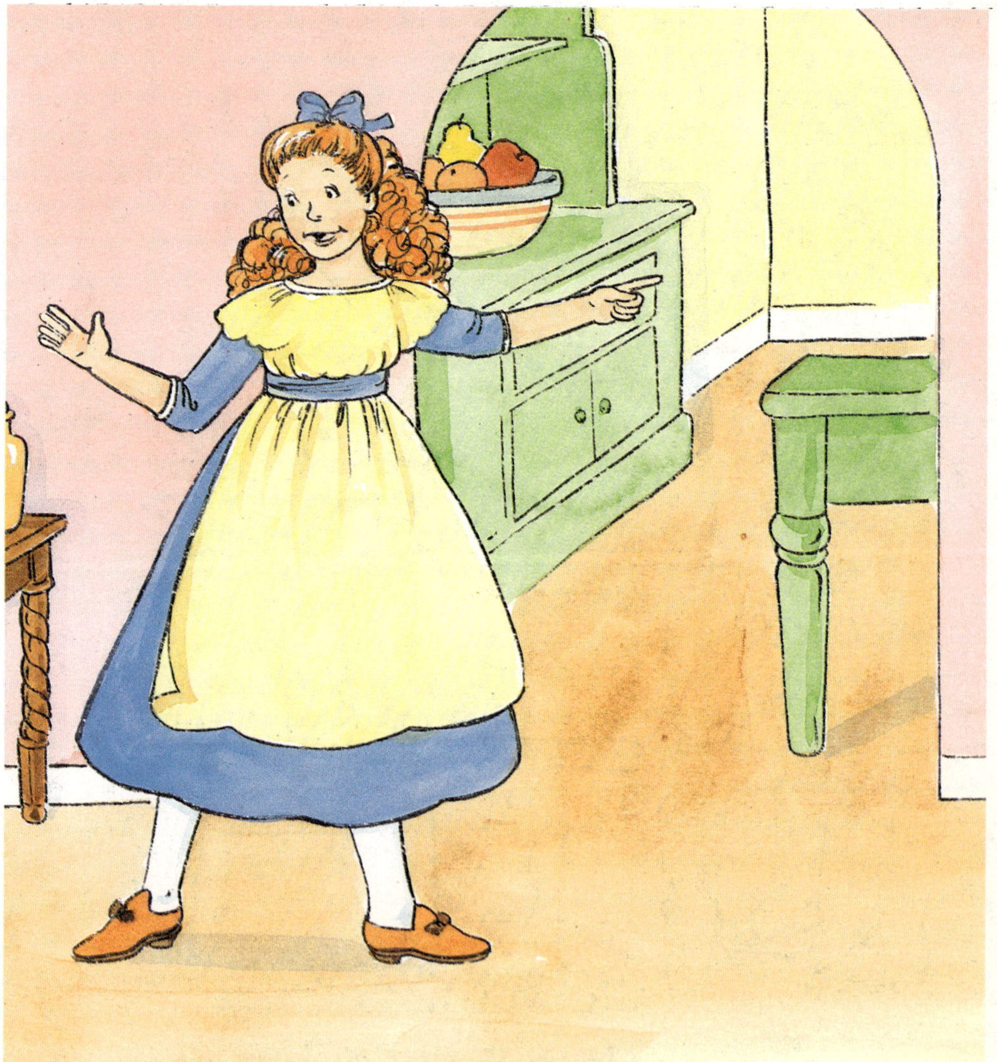

Then Sue called to June,
"This fowl is found!"

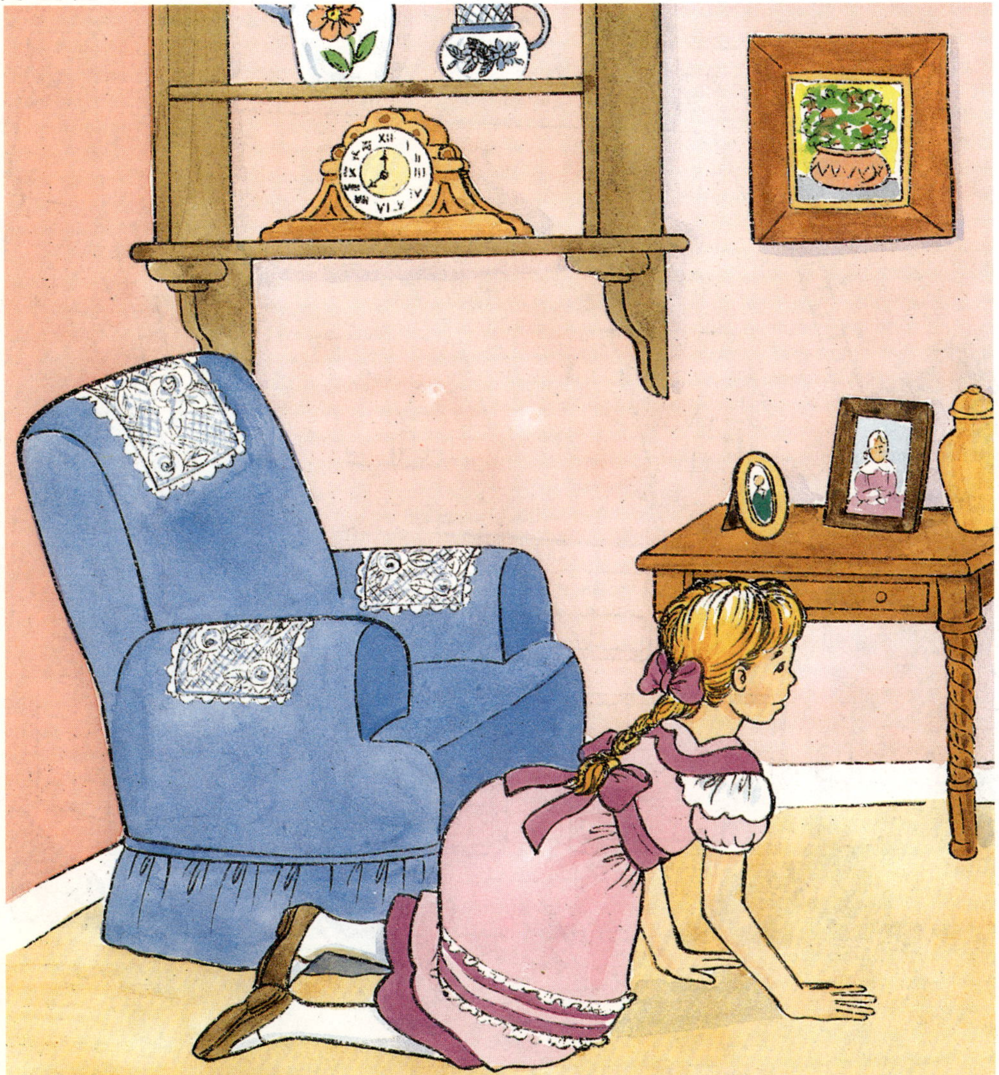

So Sue and June went in.
They looked all around.

Loose Goose Lost

Sue had a birthday.
June gave her a goose.
Sue liked her new goose.
But her new goose got loose.

That loose goose hid.
He left no clue.

"This is the last place
we can look for Stu!"

"Let's look in my house,"
said June to Sue.

He hid under a bridge.
And he hid from Sue and June.

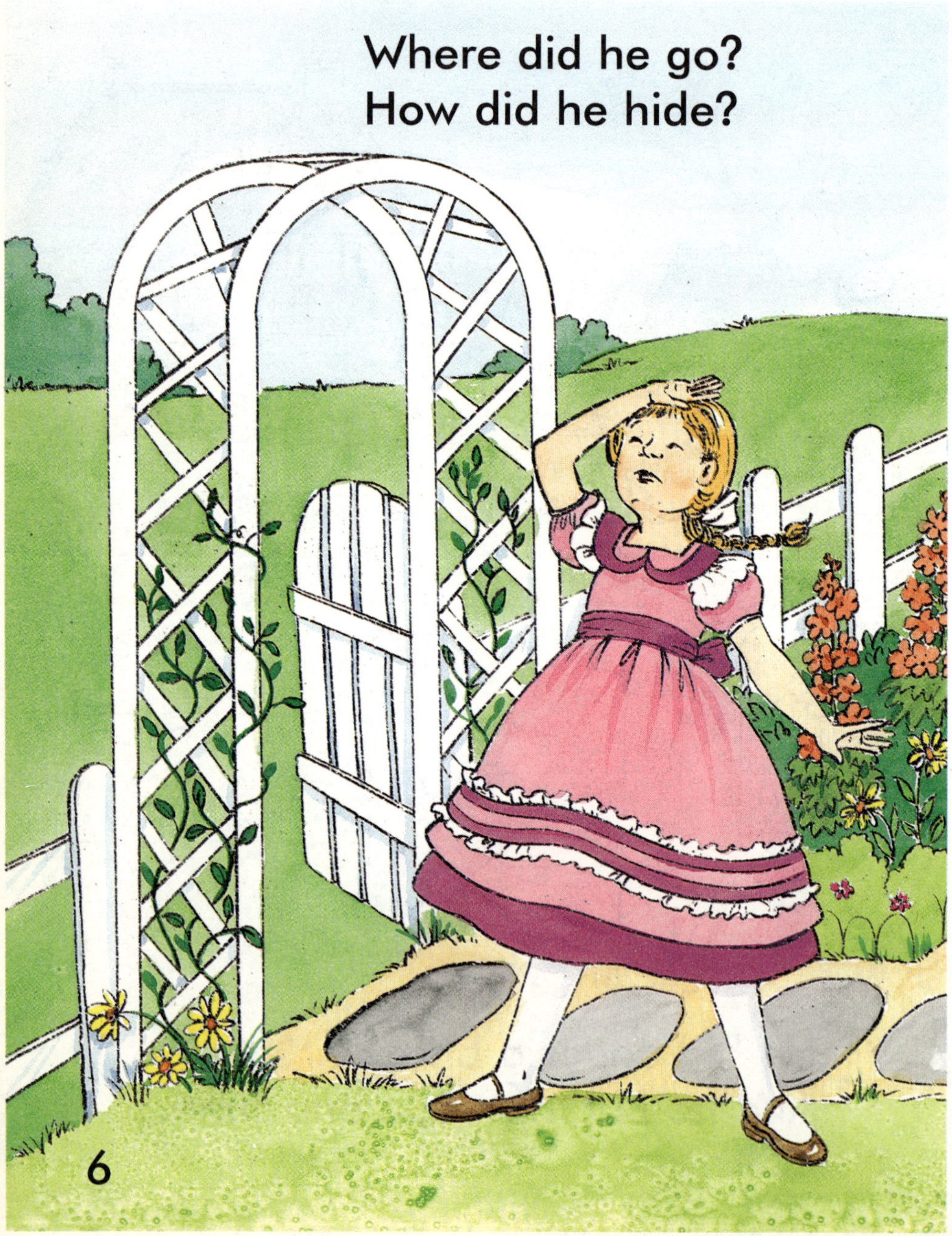

Where did he go?
How did he hide?

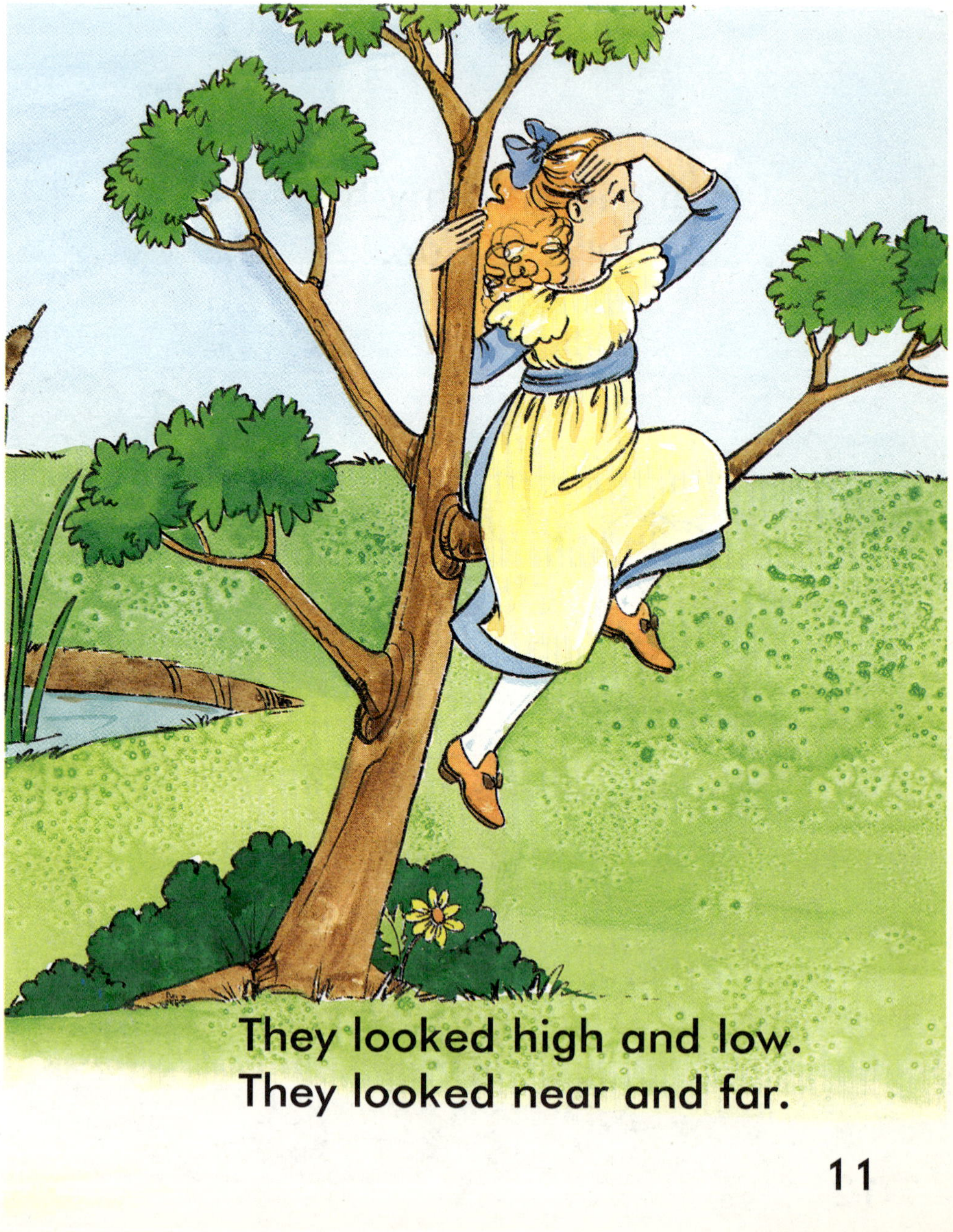

They looked high and low.
They looked near and far.

Loose Goose Found

Sue looked over here.
June looked over there.

SRA Open Court Reading

Just a moment ago,
he had been at Sue's side.

Boo hoo hoo!

So where was that goose
that Sue named "Stu"?

"This is sad!" cried June.
Sue wept, "Boo hoo hoo!"

Mom and Dad had seen, and they ran right over.
Said Tom, "I think I will name my dog Rover!"

SRA Open Court Reading

Tom's Dog

by Marilee Robin Burton
illustrated by Jan Pyk

A Division of The McGraw-Hill Companies
Columbus, Ohio

SRA/McGraw-Hill

A Division of The ***McGraw-Hill*** *Companies*

Printed in the United States of America.

Send all inquiries to:
SRA/McGraw-Hill
8787 Orion Place
Columbus, OH 43240-4027

So Tom took a deep breath.
He forgot all his fears.
He pulled out the splinter,
and then he heard cheers!

But when Tom looked again,
his dog didn't look scary.
He looked kind of scared and not at all hairy.

Mean and Scary

Mom and Dad gave a dog to Tom.
"Do you like him?" asked Tom's mom.

Tom said, "That dog is mean and scary.
He looks like a bear. He is brown and hairy."

Tom did not go near it.
He was too frightened.
A dog that was hurt could now bite him.

Tom looked a bit closer.
He saw a thorn in his dog's
hairy left paw.

"His tail is crooked. His
claws are sharp.
He has big long teeth and a
big loud bark!"

Tom got goose bumps because
he was filled with fear.
Tom ran away when that dog came near.

First his dog whimpered, and
then he started to yelp.
That's when Tom knew
that his dog needed help.

He was teaching himself a new
kickball kick.
Suddenly, he saw that his dog was sick!

Tom didn't like him, no, not at all.
Tom wished that dog was tiny
and small.

Tom saw the dog chewing his toys.
Tom began thinking, "Does he eat little boys?"

My Dog Rover

The next day Tom was out
on his own.
He was in his backyard.
He was playing alone.

It means that we can't make our dish.
Because now our dish is missing fish.

I know how we can make our dish!
Let's go shop for frozen fish!

SRA Open Court Reading

Fish Pie

by Lisa Trumbauer
illustrated by Olivia Cole

A Division of The McGraw-Hill Companies
Columbus, Ohio

SRA/McGraw-Hill
A Division of The ***McGraw-Hill*** *Companies*

Printed in the United States of America.

Send all inquiries to:
SRA/McGraw-Hill
8787 Orion Place
Columbus, OH 43240-4027

We hooked no fish, not even one.
But that's okay, we had some fun.

It's getting late. Pull up your line.
We must go back. It's rowing time.

Fish

Get up, get up, and rub both eyes.
Tonight I'm cooking you fish pies!

We must catch one fish at least,
so we can make our fish pie feast.

Still no fish? Well, that's all right.
We'll eat our food until they bite.

We make bird sounds and tell good tales.
We play the drums on our worm pails.

So grab a hat, and grab your jacket.
I will make our noon lunch and pack it.

Slimy worms that ooze make great bait. Fish love these worms and think they are great.

We sing a song, make funny faces, tap our knees, and run worm races.

Fun

We sit and wait, but that's okay.
Waiting gives us time for play.

Now grab a pole, and let's get going.
Before we fish, we do some rowing.

We row and row and row some more.
We row till we can't see the shore.

We stop the boat and knot hooks with bait.
We drop our lines, and then we wait.

The boy learned his lesson. In time, villagers stopped being angry with him and let him tend their goats. Paul became well known for speaking only the truth . . .

. . . and asking for help only when he really, truly needed it.

SRA

Open Court Reading

Wolf!

retold by Dede Mack
illustrated by Len Epstein

A Division of The McGraw·Hill Companies

Columbus, Ohio

SRA/McGraw-Hill

A Division of The McGraw-Hill Companies

Printed in the United States of America.

Send all inquiries to:
SRA/McGraw-Hill
8787 Orion Place
Columbus, OH 43240-4027

And that wolf ate up all the sheep. Paul felt awful. He had been wrong, and it was his fault.

“Wolf! Wolf!” Paul yelled again. “I mean it this time! I’m not kidding!”

Still, villagers did not budge and kept on working. The villagers would not be tricked by Paul again.

Paul Plays a Trick

Once upon a time, a boy named Paul found work taking care of a herd of sheep. Every day he took the herd to a grassy hillside. There the sheep ate their fill of sweet, green grass.

As the sheep ate, Paul played his flute and looked out for wolves. Paul knew how much wolves liked to eat sheep.

"Ha!" said a farmer. "That silly boy is tricking us again."

"I agree," another farmer stated. "But we will not be fooled this time. Let's get on with our work."

Paul Learns a Lesson

But the next day, a wolf really did come. As Paul looked on, frozen in place, a mean, hungry wolf ran after the sheep. Paul dashed to the hilltop. He took a deep breath and yelled in his loudest voice: "*Wolf!*"

"If you ever see a wolf," the villagers told him, "yell for help. We will come running."

Every day was the same as the day before. Paul played his flute and looked over the sheep as they ate grass. He looked out for wolves. But he never saw any.

The next day, Paul played the same trick. He yelled "Wolf!" and snickered when many farmers came running. Paul shouted the phrase again, "I fooled you! There is no wolf! I fooled you!"

Grumbling, the farmers went home feeling disappointed with Paul.

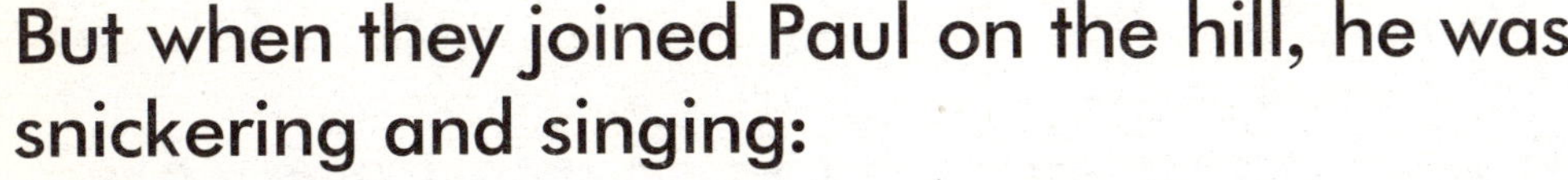

But when they joined Paul on the hill, he was snickering and singing:

"I fooled you! There is no wolf! I fooled you!"

Grumbling, the villagers went home.

"How boring this is!" sighed Paul as he yawned. "Every day is the same as before. I want to have fun."

He decided it would be fun to play a little trick on the villagers.

The next day, as the sheep were happily munching green grass, Paul dashed to the hilltop. He took a deep breath and yelled in his loudest voice: "*Wolf!*"

The villagers stopped everything and came running. "Let's go!" they cried. "We must help the boy! We must save our sheep!"

The rush is nice
but we all agree—
the hush of the night,
for us, is just right.

SRA Open Court Reading

Rush and Hush

by Reyna Eisenstark
illustrated by Kersti Frigell

A Division of The McGraw-Hill Companies
Columbus, Ohio

SRA/McGraw-Hill

A Division of The ***McGraw-Hill*** *Companies*

Printed in the United States of America.

Send all inquiries to:
SRA/McGraw-Hill
8787 Orion Place
Columbus, OH 43240-4027

Gran and I whisper and soft
meows come from Gran's cat.
A crinkle is in the pillow
where Gran's cat just sat.
Just quiet and hush here—
there is no rush here.

Gran's rocker squeaks.
A quiet rain drip-drops.
We wait for our cake
as the clock tick-tocks.

The Rush

Rush! Rush!
There is no hush here.
This is where my mom works.
She cooks while I look.

Look at them cook.
Potatoes are smashed and mashed.
Turkeys are trimmed and stuffed.
Food is squished and squashed.

Gran's cat purrs, and
Gran gives a sigh.
I hear a buzz
as a fly goes by.

We whir and stir to make a cake.
Now the cake will have to bake.
We sit and wait for our cake to bake.

Two cooks whip and stir.
Next they cut and chop.
They do not stop until it is fixed.

This is where the people eat.
Men and women crunch and chomp.
They chit and chat about this and that.

When I visit Gran, we like to bake.
Sometimes we bake a three-layer cake.
I make a little cake for my doll, Kate.

183

The Hush

Hush! Hush!
There is no rush here.
This is my mom's mom.
I call her Gran.
I see my Gran as much as I can.

Here waiters zip
and zig and zag.
Waiters rush and dash.
Oh, no! They crash!

Look out! A large plate tips!
There is an oops, an eek, a crash,
and then a big SMASH.

Both waiters fall and tumble.
Dishes clang, bang, and clatter.
"Waiter, can you rush?"
It is not quiet here.

Three hot kids—
A boy and two girls—
Sailed off into the sunset
And went around the world!

SRA Open Court Reading

A Cool Plan

by Jessica Slote
illustrated by Olivia Cole

A Division of The McGraw·Hill Companies
Columbus, Ohio

SRA/McGraw-Hill

A Division of The **McGraw-Hill** *Companies*

Printed in the United States of America.

Send all inquiries to:
SRA/McGraw-Hill
8787 Orion Place
Columbus, OH 43240-4027

Three hot kids
Had a cool plan.
They put their heads together
And made a big fan.

Mom and Dad
Pay us a visit.
"What did you make?" they ask.
"Just what is it?"

We made a ship,
Just us three.
Dad nods and smiles,
"Oh! Now we see!"

Find It

Three hot kids,
Art, Nan, and Moon,
Couldn't think of what to do
On this hot afternoon.

Ping-Pong? Catch?
No way, it's just too hot!
Who can budge? Who wants to?
We are stuck to this spot.

Mom has been outside,
Cutting pieces of wood.
"Can we have some?" asks Moon.
"Maybe wood would be good."

Up goes our flag.
Don't let it rip!
Soon we will sail
In our sailing ship!

That plank of wood
Goes over this box.
Now paint a drawing
On those old socks!

Shift that sheet to the right.
Let that sheet catch the air.
Hang that wheel in the tree.
Put that box over there.

Three hot kids
Decide there's a way
To have fun together
On a sticky, summer day.

Look! Stop! Wait!
Did you see that sheet?
A big white sheet
Would really be so neat!

Dad's clean sheets
Hang on the line.
Art asks, "Can we use one?"
Dad says, "That is fine."

Put Dad's sheet up
So no one will see
What this fantastic thing
Will turn out to be.

191

Make It

The heat is forgotten
—it's 90 degrees!
Moon, Nan, and Art
Set up camp by a tree.

They have a wheel, a rope,
Paint in a pail,
A plank, a few pins,
And a sheet for a sail.

Three hot kids
Are all set for some fun.
Dad gives them a few pins, too.
They thank him and run.

See that man's yard sale?
Where the rack of ties is?
I see cans of paint and rope
And pails in different sizes.

Three hot kids
With a cool plan.
Get out some change and pay the price.
And then they thank the man.

Let's spread out our stuff
Right here in a ring.
How can we use these little things
To make one big thing?

"It's the party crew with
mops, brooms, and pails.
Now we can have a cleaning party!
I have the best pals!"

SRA Open Court Reading

Richy Raccoon's Party

by Lisa Trumbauer
illustrated by Deborah Colvin Borgo

A Division of The McGraw-Hill Companies

Columbus, Ohio

Open Court Reading

SRA/McGraw-Hill

A Division of The ***McGraw-Hill*** *Companies*

Printed in the United States of America.

Send all inquiries to:
SRA/McGraw-Hill
8787 Orion Place
Columbus, OH 43240-4027

"Whoops!" shrieks Richy Raccoon.
"This party was fun,
but, oh, what a mess! Hmm,
someone is knocking at my door."

"Bart, that birthday cake was the best. We ate every last crumb!"

Birthday Surprise

"Is this a birthday party for me?" Richy Raccoon waves to his friends.

"Surprise," yells Bart Bear.
"I was in charge of the cake.
I hope you like chewy fudge."

"See you later, skunks.
Thank you for bringing ice cream!
Not a spoonful is left!"

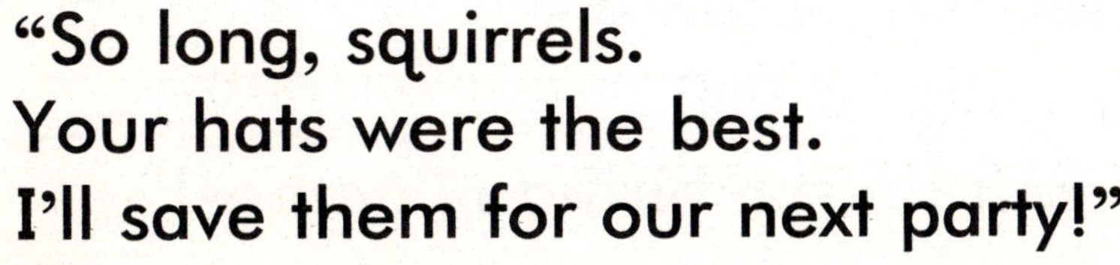

"So long, squirrels.
Your hats were the best.
I'll save them for our next party!"

Sammy and Sue Skunk bring
Richy's favorite ice creams,
a quart of mint and
a quart of gooey grape.

The squirrels bring birthday hats!
"Let's all put on a hat," says Richy Raccoon.
"We still have more surprises," squealed Charlie Squirrel.

"I will see you soon,
Freddie and family!
Thank you for my birthday games!"

"Thanks for my birthday party! Good-bye, ducks. I really liked my balloons!"

The Frog Family brings
in beach balls.
"Now we can play party
games!" shouts Freddie Frog.

“The Ducklings are holding balloons in their beaks!” shouts Richy Raccoon. “I see red, yellow, green, and blue balloons!”

“What a great party! I have cake, ice cream, hats, balls, and balloons!” cries Richy Raccoon. “And the best part of all—my friends!”

Now that you know a few ways animals hide, look at this picture again. How many animals can you find now?

SRA Open Court Reading

Animals That Hide

by Doria Romero
illustrated by Meryl Henderson

A Division of The McGraw-Hill Companies
Columbus, Ohio

SRA/McGraw-Hill
A Division of The ***McGraw-Hill*** *Companies*

Printed in the United States of America.

Send all inquiries to:
SRA/McGraw-Hill
8787 Orion Place
Columbus, OH 43240-4027

or in white snow? Why?

If this rabbit needed to hide, would it hide in brown dirt . . .

How many animals can you find in this picture?

Animals sometimes need to hide. They hide to catch food to eat and to keep from being eaten. Each has its own way to hide and blend in with its background.

Sea Animals

Some whales are lighter on the bottom and darker on top. If you are under this whale, it looks like a patch of light.

The bug in this picture is called a walking stick. Can you find it? How do you think it got its name?

A tiger is the same color as the grass and sticks around it. How does this help it hide?

If you are over this whale, it looks like a patch of dark sand.

Many starfish look just like plants. There are three starfish in this picture. Can you find them?

There is a butterfly in this picture. It looks like a leaf. Can you find it?

Land Animals

Snakes are the same color as the things around them. This helps them blend in. How many snakes can you find?

Have you ever covered yourself with sand at a beach? Rays hide by covering up with sand.

A flounder is flat and can hide on the sea bottom. What else helps a flounder hide?

Reefs are chains of rocks and animals.
Many sea animals hide in reefs.
How many fish can you find in this reef?